Bewilder the Dragon

Negotiating amongst confusion

Bewilder the Dragon

Negotiating amongst confusion

Leonie McKeon

DoctorZed
Publishing
www.doctorzed.com

Copyright © 2020 by Leonie McKeon

All rights reserved. No part of this book may be used or reproduced by any means, graphic, electronic, or mechanical, including photocopying, recording, taping or by any information storage retrieval system without the written permission of the publisher except in the case of brief quotations embodied in critical articles and reviews.

Books may be ordered through booksellers or by contacting: www.leoniemckeon.com

1st edition published by DoctorZed Publishing www.doctorzed.com

ISBN: 978-0-6481315-0-2 (hc)
ISBN: 978-0-6481314-8-9 (sc)
ISBN: 978-0-6481314-9-6 (ebk)

A CiP number for this title can be found at the National Library of Australia.

Cover image © Trish Pollock

Because of the dynamic nature of the Internet, any web addresses or links contained in this book may have changed since publication and may no longer be valid. The views expressed in this work are solely those of the author. The author does not dispense financial advice or prescribe the use of any technique as a form of guarantee for financial or business viability without the advice of a qualified financial advisor, either directly or indirectly. The intent of the author is only to offer information of a general nature to help you in your business. In the event you use any of the information in this book for yourself or your business, which is your constitutional right, the author and the publisher assume no responsibility for your actions.

Printed in Australia, UK and USA.
rev. date 12/02/2020

Contents

Acknowledgements

*I*t is only with the support of so many different people that I am able to conclude this fourth book in *The Dao of Negotiation: The Path Between Eastern strategies and Western minds*. I want to thank my publisher Dr. Scott Zarcinas at DoctorZed Publishing, my editor Hari Teah, and my designer Trish Pollock at BrandArk, all of whom have contributed their skills to the publication of this book. I particularly want to thank Kate Lyall whose excellent research skills have made such a positive contribution to *Bewilder the Dragon: Negotiating amongst Confusion*. My sister Jennifer McKeon has provided unlimited faith and belief in me and the project, as well as continuing to read and re-read drafts. Finally, I want to thank organisational psychologist Shelley Rogers who has helped me think through the complexities of many of the examples. More importantly, Shelley remains entirely supportive of me and *The Dao of Negotiation* project, for which I am endlessly appreciative.

"*Let your plans be dark and impenetrable as night, and when you move, fall like a thunderbolt.*"

Sun Tzu, *The Art of War*

Leonie's Journey Continues

After living overseas for eight years I returned and relocated to Adelaide, South Australia. My plan was to go to university, however I had to defer that plan for a year because I realised I did not have the necessary skills to do a university degree. Although I had expected Australia to have changed in a physical sense, after a couple of months I realised Australia had changed more linguistically. Popular culture had shifted and new words had come into the language. I then understood that every language evolves as the culture shifts. My Mandarin Chinese was excellent. My English, on the other hand, was where it had been eight years before when I left Australia. So I enrolled in the final year of high school in an adult entry college where I studied subjects requiring considerable written work, because I knew I needed this practice. During that year of studying, it was not only the linguistic differences that I noticed; the physical differences also caught my attention. As I walked around the streets I was fascinated by how the houses all looked so different from one another, because I had been living in high rise apartments in Taiwan for the past five years, where apartments all looked the same from the outside. In supermarkets everyone seemed so loud because I could understand everything people were saying. And I could read everything on the supermarket shelves. My eyes had adjusted to seeing Chinese faces, so for the first few months everyone in Australia looked the same. After a year of studying English and history in the adult entry college, I commenced my university degree, studying anthropology and Mandarin. Anthropology provided me with the lenses to see ideas in many different ways. As I was very competent in Mandarin I was placed straight into the second year of the course. I was disappointed by the way Mandarin was taught, and realised why very few non-Chinese people did this course. It was set up to be difficult, and from studying anthropology and understanding how discourses are created, it was obvious that this course was not designed to help non-native Chinese speakers succeed. At the end of my university degree, I decided to create a new discourse, which would be 'Mandarin is not difficult, it is just different.' After I completed my university degree I applied for an entrepreneurial scholarship with the University of Adelaide, with the aim of implementing this discourse. I won this scholarship in 1998.

Introduction to Confucianism

The Confucian tradition and philosophy is a way of life for many Chinese people. It is based on the teachings of Confucius, a Chinese philosopher who was born in the Shandong Province (the feudal state Lu), in the 6th to 5th century BCE. Confucianism is not a religion, although the teachings of Confucius have had a strong and enduring impact on the life, social structure, political philosophy and civilisation of China. Confucian teachings have transformed over time, and even today they remain a foundation for the values that underpin the social code of Chinese people. Some of the core values in Confucianism include respect and reverence for family, parents, and elders; reciprocity in relationships, and caring for others.

Understanding Confucianism helps to understand the social rules in your business interactions with Chinese people. In the Confucian tradition, rituals are used in all aspects of social life, from important events such as births, weddings, and funerals, to everyday interactions. Ritual is used to establish an orderly, harmonious, and prosperous society. In the practice of Confucianism each interaction is perceived as an opportunity to strive for moral excellence. In Book Two – *Deceive The Dragon: Negotiating to retain power*, the concept of *guanxi*, which is about connections, is introduced. Understanding *guanxi* helps us to comprehend that the foundation of Chinese business culture is personal relationships. Book Three – *Lure The Tiger: Negotiation in confronting circumstances*, explores the concept of 'face'. Within relationships, Chinese people give and receive 'face' from one another as a way of showing respect. Confucianism builds on these concepts and ties them together.

Confusion Strategies

*J*n Book Four – *Bewilder the Dragon: Negotiating amongst confusion,* you will learn six strategies that use confusion to the strategist's advantage. This book will describe Strategies 19 - 24 that are used when you are facing a stronger opponent and cannot compete directly. Knowledge of the **Confusion Strategies** will allow you to create and take advantage of uncertain situations.

Strategies 19 - 24 are used by a strategist to reduce the strength of their opponent. They can be used to unbalance, bewilder, and disorientate adversaries, thus making it difficult for them to focus and to act decisively. The aim of the **Confusion Strategies** is to create more favourable conditions for the strategist to move within. These are achieved by attacking the material and psychological resources of adversaries, using surprise to your advantage, and creating illusions to mystify and hinder their ability to move against you. Book Four – *Bewilder the Dragon: Negotiating amongst confusion* will explore these strategies, and teach you how to guard against Strategies 19 - 24, and also how to find opportunities within uncertain situations.

Confusion
Strategies

Steal the firewood from under the pot
means "to eliminate the source of strength"

When faced with an enemy too powerful to engage directly, you must first weaken him by undermining his foundation and attacking his source of power.

Cao Cao had commenced a military campaign against General Yuan Shao to gain access to a piece of valuable territory. General Xu Yu, who was an expert strategist, joined Cao Cao on this campaign. General Xu Yu initially wanted to assess the situation by meeting with Cao Cao and enquiring about how the military campaign was progressing. He was concerned because this campaign appeared to be going on for a long time. His main enquiry was about the state of Cao Cao's supplies. Cao Cao was quite anxious about the situation and told General Xu Yu that his people only had approximately one month's worth of supplies left, while General Yuan Shao had enough supplies to last his people a year. This was a problem, because there seemed to be no end in sight to this military campaign. At this stage it was obvious that General Yuan Shao would win the campaign because he had an abundance of supplies. It was very clear to General Xu Yu that Cao Cao would not be able to defeat General Yuan Shao unless they *'attacked his source of power'*. This source of power was General Yuan Shao's provisions. To eliminate General Yuan Shao's provisions, General Xu Yu applied Strategy Nineteen – **Steal the firewood from under the pot**.

In order to apply Strategy Nineteen, General Xu Yu devised a plan. He had a number of troops dressed to look like the soldiers of General Yuan Shao's army. The disguised soldiers rode horses to General Yuan Shao's soldiers' garrison, where their food was stored. They placed cloth on the hooves of their horses to travel quietly, and because they looked like General Yuan Shao's soldiers they did not attract attention. If anyone was suspicious they said they were patrolling the area as directed by General Yuan Shao. When they reached the food supplies they set the garrison on fire and rode away.

Once General Yuan Shao found out what had happened to his provisions, he immediately comprehended that he and his men were at risk of starvation, as they now had no food left, and would therefore not be able to continue with the campaign. After three days General Yuan Shao's troops were weak, as they had not eaten, and they quickly lost their motivation to fight any longer. Cao Cao won the campaign and gained access to the valuable territory.

When Strategy Nineteen is used, the strategist determines the source of their competitor's strength and focuses on eliminating this strength, which eliminates their competitor's advantage.

Negotiating with Chinese People

EXAMPLE ONE
Strategy Nineteen in action (against you)

When Strategy Nineteen is used on you, the strategist carefully uses the strategy to attack a valuable resource. The strategist has done their research and is fully aware you do not have a backup for this most significant resource.

Strategy Nineteen is specifically about your *'source of power'* being eliminated. When conducting business with China, if you are not a Mandarin Chinese speaker, you will be faced with a language barrier. Even though there are many people in China who have experienced a Western education, there is still a large part of the population which has limited English. To deal with this language barrier foreign companies often employ a Chinese staff member.

Imagine the company you manage is a training organisation that specialises in project management and other areas regarding human resources. You have completed your market research, and it is apparent the skills of the training organisation you manage are highly sought-after in China. Your company is quite large and has solid resources, so you therefore feel that your size will protect you from any strategies put in place by Chinese companies to extract your highly sought-after intellectual property. You have employed one Chinese staff member, who you feel is very capable and also very loyal to you, and so you are confident they will not leave for some years.

Your company is too big for a Chinese company to compete with, and therefore your Chinese competitors feel you are *'too powerful to engage directly'*, so they apply Strategy Nineteen to *'undermine your foundation and attack your source of power'*. You do not realise that, in this case, your 'source of power' is your Chinese staff member, and you have no backup if this staff member leaves the company. They are your *'source of power'* because your Chinese staff member does all of your translations and interpretations.

They are also a significant component in your China visits, to help you with meetings and other cultural and linguistic areas. Your Chinese staff member has translated your training materials, so they know all the intricate details of the courses. Most of your client base is in the hospitality area, in large hotel chains in Shanghai, and your Chinese staff member has developed solid *guanxi* with many of these people.

On one of your trips to Shanghai your competitor strategically puts Strategy Nineteen in place and begins to '*attack your source of power*' by encouraging your Chinese staff member to work for their company. Your competitor has been strategically researching your progression in the China market, and has waited until the right time to offer your Chinese staff member a position in their company. They offer an attractive salary combined with excellent incentives. Your competitor is aware your Chinese staff member has their family in Shanghai, and that they come from the generation of the 'one child family policy'. Therefore this person has a high level of responsibility towards looking after their family. Your competitor offers them a position in Shanghai with a once-a-year offshore professional development course for a period of five days in the country of their choice. For your Chinese employee this is an offer too good to refuse, and they accept the position. By doing this, your competitor has applied Strategy Nineteen and eliminated '*your source of power*'.

In this situation, without your key resource, your business in China will suffer. Your competitor now has your Chinese staff member, who is someone who knows your training material and has strong *guanxi* with your contacts. This will create a significant deficit for your business, and it will be difficult in the short-term for your training organisation to operate successfully in China.

EXAMPLE ONE
Guarding yourself against Strategy Nineteen

There is no doubt that having a Chinese staff member to assist you in dealing with your clients and contacts when you travel to China is a great asset. For you to guard yourself against Strategy Nineteen being successfully applied on you, it is a good idea not to position your Chinese staff member as your '*source of power*'. Remove the focus from them as being such a key resource by delegating some of the critical tasks to other people. It is often easy to get caught up in allowing your Chinese staff member to assist you with everything to do with China. Having some understanding of Mandarin Chinese is a great asset. However, if you have no time to learn Mandarin, it is a good idea to learn the basics - which is to pronounce Pinyin. When you understand Pinyin you can read Chinese names, street signs, and many other things that are written in Pinyin. Even though it appears to be a good idea to get your Chinese employee to do some or all translating of materials, to guard yourself against Strategy Nineteen it would be clever to outsource all translation jobs which include your training materials. Although this may be slightly more expensive, in the long-term it is beneficial because it means that your Chinese staff member is not fully versed in all the language, concepts, and methodology of your training materials. To further guard yourself against Strategy Nineteen being applied, when your

Chinese staff member is diligently developing *guanxi* with the hotel managers and other relevant people, you need to be attending all of the meetings with them, to develop your own *guanxi*. This is not a time to be complacent; rather it is a time to keep abreast of everything that is going on around you.

Example Two
Strategy Nineteen in action (against you)

You own a company that sells commercial air-conditioning units and you have been getting your air-conditioning units made in a factory in China for five years. In your opinion things have been going well. You perceive your customers as your '*source of power*'. You come to this conclusion because without your customers you see you have no business. You have been cautious not to divulge any information about your customers to the factory you deal with in China. Your customers are located all over the world. You have three different unit designs, the components for which are all manufactured in one factory in China, before being sent back to your country to be assembled. This has worked well, because the quality of all the components is checked thoroughly, assembled in your country, then sent off to your customers. As you see your customers as your '*source of power*' you are careful to look after them. Over the last five years of doing business in China, you have developed solid *guanxi*, and the quality of the product is checked in your own country. So when it fails to meet your high standards and there is a faulty product, you are able to fix the issue easily. As you have all product components made in one factory in China, the senior people in that factory have access to all the designs. Even so, you do not see this as a problem. They are aware you have a unique product, and that the technology to operate this product has been invented by you. Other people who deal with China have forewarned you that you are likely to have your intellectual property copied in China. However, you strongly believe that your solid *guanxi* will guard you against this.

In the sixth year of your business you notice that your client base has slightly declined. The reason for this decline is that the senior people in the factory in China that you deal with have copied your intellectual property and sold this to another company in China, which has captured some of your customer base. The company has a joint venture agreement with an American company, and because the company is based in China, they do not have any of the costs of sending the product to America for checking, as this is all done in China. They are able to send the air-conditioning units directly to the customer from China, which is a big cost saving. Once everything had been established, the company located some of your customers and offered them identical units at a cheaper price. They successfully applied Strategy Nineteen by '*undermining your foundation and attacking your source of power*'.

Example Two
Guarding yourself against Strategy Nineteen

Protecting your intellectual property can be challenging when you do business in China. Sometimes all the effort you apply can be wasted energy, as there is always a risk of it being stolen. So it is wise to understand that you are not going to change the way Chinese business people think about intellectual property. Making money is very important for Chinese business people. There is nothing wrong with this way of thinking. However, it is important to understand that they will go to great lengths to achieve this goal. Even if you do not agree with their perspective regarding intellectual property, it is better to figure out a way of operating inside this way of thinking. In the case of the air-conditioning company, they could guard themselves against Strategy Nineteen by spreading the manufacturing across three different factories in three different provinces throughout China. In this way, it would be difficult for anyone to copy all the technology for the air-conditioning units, because anyone who tried to copy the design would only have one third of the product. Guarding yourself in this way helps reduce the risk that your manufacturers will be able to copy the product technology, because each factory never has access to the whole product.

Key Points when Strategy Nineteen is used against you

- To retain your source of power, never rely on one Chinese employee as the main resource. Delegate some responsibilities to others to avoid one employee attaining all of your company secrets.
- Understand where the source of your power really lies.
- When working with manufacturers, spread different manufacturing processes across separate companies based in different regions to protect your intellectual property.

Example Three
Enacting Strategy Nineteen

A scenario where you can apply Strategy Nineteen may be where you are a company that has a joint venture with a hotel in China. The hotel is a four-star hotel, and is in the popular tourist city of Xi'an, home of the Terracotta Warriors. There are many foreign tourists keen to visit the Terracotta Warriors. You observe that many of the tours do not meet the needs of foreigners, due to language barriers, as tour operators lack adequate English language skills. Your biggest competitor is a four-and-a-half star hotel, which is a kilometre away from your hotel's location. This competitor hotel is very large and grand, and is wholly Chinese-owned. They pride themselves on luxurious rooms with spectacular views and a very grand dining room. This hotel's owners are concerned about 'face'.

You have visited this hotel and realise you cannot compete directly because it is so large. When you visited the hotel you noticed the ten tour operators positioned at desks in the foyer, and noted how they communicated with foreigners. Their customer service skills impressed you, and five of these tour operators spoke very good English. You are also aware that this hotel has internal conflicts inside the management team. You know this because a member of staff who recently came to work at your hotel left your competitor's hotel as a result of these internal conflicts. By watching this situation unfold from afar you apply Strategy Nine – **Watching the fire from the opposite shore** from Book Two – *Deceive the Dragon: Negotiating to retain power*.

To apply Strategy Nineteen you develop your knowledge about the disarray in the other hotel's management team. You see the English-speaking tour operators are their '*source of power*', whereas the other hoteliers' see their hotel's ambiance and furnishings as their '*source of power*'. They are so focused on providing 'face' that they do not see the assets they have in the tour operators. To apply Strategy Nineteen you invite the five best tour operators to an upmarket restaurant and discuss with them the possibility of their working for your hotel. You know they are unhappy at their present location, as a result of the hotel's internal management disputes. You offer them a commission that is ten percent higher than what they are currently receiving, plus weekly English classes. They take up your offer, and your hotel is then able to offer excellent tours with English-speaking tour guides.

By offering the tour operators a good deal, which they accept, you successfully apply Strategy Nineteen by attacking your competitor's '*source of power*'.

Negotiating in a Western Environment

EXAMPLE FOUR
Enacting Strategy Nineteen

In this scenario you have applied for an internal promotion. You know that a colleague of yours has also applied, which means that you both have interviews coming up for this position. In your preparation for the interview you research the people who have been chosen to sit on the interview panel. You also research your competitor's background and discover that your competitor and one of the panel members worked together at a previous company, and know each other quite well. You are concerned that this may give them an advantage over you at the interview. In this situation their relationship with a panel member is their '*source of power*'. To weaken your competitor you choose to '*undermine their foundation*', by contacting your organisation's human resources department and enquiring as to whether this pre-existing relationship could create a conflict of interest for the panel member. The human resources department decided that it could be seen as unfair treatment, and therefore appoints a different person, which means your competitor's '*source of power*' has been replaced by a person they do not know. By having the panel member removed, you have removed the '*source of your competitor's power*' without '*engaging them directly*', and they no longer have an advantage over you.

Key Points when using Strategy Nineteen

- Research your competition to understand their source of power.
- Determine what your competitor's weaknesses and vulnerabilities are.
- Exposing your competitor's weaknesses will enable you to remove their source of power.

Trouble the water to catch the fish *means* "to create confusion and make your move while others are distracted"

Before engaging your enemy's forces create confusion to weaken his perception and judgment. Do something unusual, strange and unexpected as this will arouse the enemy's suspicion and disrupt his thinking. A distracted enemy is more vulnerable.

---

*G*eneral Jin Di wanted to attack the territory of Wu. To instigate this attack, he sent an army of 200,000 soldiers, led by his great strategist, Du Yu. When these soldiers arrived outside the main city of Yue Siang, which was situated next to the Xangze River, Du Yu applied Strategy Twenty - **Trouble the water to catch the fish** by '*creating confusion to weaken the Wu soldiers' perception and judgement.*' He did this by ordering his captain to secretly cross the river with just 200 soldiers. When they crossed the river they were in close proximity to Yue Siang, where they changed into uniforms that looked like those of the Wu army.

They did this because Du Yu wanted to do something '*strange and unexpected to disrupt the Wu army's thinking*'. The 200 soldiers were disguised to look like the Wu army, and then hid themselves near the city, waiting to ambush.

Meanwhile, the general who was in charge of the Wu territory found out about General Jin Di's plan to attack the city of Yue Siang and directed his army to go into battle against the Jin Di soldiers. The Wu army was able to stop General Jin Di's soldiers from entering the city of Yue Siang. However, when the Wu soldiers returned to their city, the Jin Di soldiers who were waiting in ambush mixed themselves amongst the Wu army which '*disrupted the Wu army's thinking*' because they could not distinguish between who was part of their army and who was part of the Wu army. These 200 Jin Di soldiers '*took advantage of the situation*' by lighting fires all over Yue Siang. '*Confusion was created*', and in the chaos the rest of the Jin Di soldiers entered the city of Yue Siang and conquered the Wu army, taking over the city.

In this situation, Jin Di's strategist Du Yu applied Strategy Twenty. By doing something unexpected which '*created confusion*', he was then able to take advantage of the chaos. The purpose of the application of Strategy Twenty is to '*create confusion*', and then to take advantage of the chaotic situation.

Negotiating with Chinese People

EXAMPLE ONE
Strategy Twenty in action (against you)

You import furniture from China, supplying a large retail outlet in your country. You have been doing business with China for five years and have established solid *guanxi*, with a factory in Hangzhou, China. To develop this relationship you have worked very hard by going back and forth to China in order to meet the right people. There are three furniture products that you supply that are manufactured in China, which are coffee tables, kitchen chairs, and kitchen tables. Over a five-year period you have established a strong relationship with your Chinese manufacturers, and you now have the standard of quality you want for your products.

On a routine visit to the factory where you are introducing a seasonal design variation to your product range required by your client in your home country, you meet with your usual contact. At the point when you think you have everything in place to ensure sure the manufacture of this design variation, they apply Strategy Twenty to *'create confusion and weaken your perception and judgement'* by presenting several new drawings and prices, and saying nothing. They are aware this will make you *'distracted'* and you will be *'more vulnerable'*. The prices they have prepared are higher than you have previously discussed, and they validate this by saying materials have risen in price.

Example One
Guarding yourself against Strategy Twenty

To guard yourself against Strategy Twenty be aware that even though you have a strong relationship, when dealing with Chinese people you are dealing with expert negotiators. Even if you have something out of the ordinary presented to you, the most useful reaction is to stay calm, as this is a strategy applied to confuse you. You can wait. You do not have to make a decision in the middle of this confusion, because it is likely to be detrimental to the overall outcome you want.

To guard yourself against Strategy Twenty, you would benefit from having more than one supplier, and ideally in different provinces. In this situation you may say this proposal does not suit your budget and you will seek out some other manufacturers. To save 'face' mention that it has been a pleasure dealing with them, and assure them that you fully understand the situation.

EXAMPLE TWO
Strategy Twenty in action (against you)

You are very successful in the coffee shop business in your own country, and you have heard coffee shop culture has become a popular activity in China, particularly in Shanghai. So you perceive there to be an opportunity in China for you to expand your business. In your home country you have been in the coffee business for 20 years, and you own and operate upmarket coffee shops. To get introduced to some potential business opportunities in China you join a government delegation to visit China, which your home city is organising. You are looking for a Chinese partner to launch a joint venture with, so you can bring your coffee business knowledge to China. The plan is to use your expertise in the coffee business, and your Chinese business partner will know good locations, government connections, and the rules and regulations to operate in China. You meet several Chinese business people on this trip to China. There is one Chinese group that you feel you have a good connection with. However, your concern is that they know very little about the coffee business. In spite of this, you decide there is no need for concern because by approaching the project as a joint venture they have applied Strategy Twelve - **Seize the opportunity to lead a sheep away** from Book Two – *Deceive the Dragon: Negotiating to retain power*. This is where Chinese people are seeking every opportunity, and it is not necessary to have expertise in the area they are looking to engage with. They are interested in dealing with foreign business people, and have the necessary contacts to pave the way to open up coffee shops in Shanghai.

After visiting China you are feeling happy that you have met with a potential Chinese business partner. You return to your home country. After a couple of weeks of constant communication with your Chinese contact you decide that this group will be a good fit for a joint venture. You spend time preparing everything you need for the joint venture, which includes trademarking your brand in the region and organising for the specialised coffee to be sent to China. Even though nothing has been signed, all parties are quite confident this will be a productive joint venture. Your new partners organise your hotel in Shanghai, where you are having meetings every day. Their English is good, which is a bonus, because you do not speak any Mandarin Chinese. You have been taken to several locations in Shanghai to choose the most suitable venues for the coffee shops, and you decide on two of these locations. After four weeks of meetings you sign the joint venture agreement. Although the agreement does not state the exact locations of the planned coffee shops, you assume that they will be in Shanghai, as this is where you have been looking. During the last three days of your China visit your joint venture partners offer to take you sightseeing. Agreements have been signed, locations have been chosen, and construction dates have been decided on. After a couple of days of sightseeing you feel quite exhausted, and in this scenario Strategy Four – **Wait leisurely for an exhausted enemy** from Book One – *Tame the Tiger: Negotiating from a position of power* is being applied. This is in preparation for the application of Strategy Twenty. When you are on a boat travelling on the Huang Pu River – also known as The Yellow River – your new partner applies Strategy Twenty. Your Chinese partners imply that a further agreement after the first year means the expansion of coffee shops across all of China, which means exclusivity. This was never discussed. To apply Strategy Twenty they '*disrupt your thinking*' by doing '*something unusual, strange, and unexpected*'. As exclusivity is something that you are aware will link you with only one business partner for the whole of China, you are placed in a difficult situation. Also, you are leaving China the next day and feel there is no time to discuss this further. They are quite clear that exclusivity is the best option, as this will give you all much more scope. You have spent a lot of time and energy getting to this point, and to undo this would be such a difficult task. Even though exclusivity is a risk, you feel it is better for you to agree to this option, although it will limit you to one joint venture partner. By accepting the consequences of Strategy Twenty you have taken a risky path in China for your business venture.

Example Two
Guarding yourself against Strategy Twenty

In this situation, to guard yourself against Strategy Twenty it would have been beneficial to spend more time conducting research into the potential of a wider range of business opportunities in China. As the coffee drinking culture in Shanghai has grown, there are likely to be several Chinese business people interested in what you have to offer. Understand that Strategy Twelve - **Seize the opportunity to lead a sheep away** is likely to be in action whenever you speak with Chinese business people. Chinese people see the knowledge of conducting business as being more important than experience in the business you have to offer. Having no knowledge of the coffee shop industry will be normal, and when you understand this thinking you can widen your options when choosing a joint venture partner, because several Chinese business people who have good connections may be potential joint venture partners. Since coffee drinking culture is becoming popular in China you would be wise to research what is already there. Speak to people who are already operating similar businesses in China, such as coffee shops and wine bars. People who are foreigners to China and have already launched joint ventures with

Chinese businesses are wonderful sources of information. It is quite common for Chinese business people to want exclusivity for the whole of China, because this is a way of excluding Chinese business people in other provinces across China. Exclusivity should therefore be one of the first issues up for discussion.

Take your time and try to think of all possible options, and do your research. You may trust and feel comfortable with your Chinese business partner. Even so, keep in mind that you are dealing with skilful business people who are likely to manipulate a situation by applying Strategy Twenty. To guard yourself against the successful application of Strategy Twenty it is important to predict what your Chinese business partners want, and in this case it is exclusivity. This is not about distrusting your joint venture partner; rather it is about knowing how to play the game of business with them.

Key Points when Strategy Twenty is used against you

- When dealing with Chinese business people, stay calm and take your time when presented with something out of the ordinary.
- Select a number of Chinese business partners to avoid being trapped into an exclusive business relationship.
- Avoid sharing your complete travel itinerary with your Chinese business partners.

EXAMPLE THREE
Enacting Strategy Twenty

A situation could be that you run a business that works in early learning for young children, and your research suggests this has become a popular business in China. You have set up a joint venture with an early learning centre in Beijing, which is a great opportunity because they have the contacts and location already set up and you have the curriculum that is a hybrid program of Western and Chinese education, so this is an equal partnership. Through previous meetings, networking, and attending exhibitions, you have met a Chinese contact with whom you perceive a possible joint venture to establish an early learning centre in Kunming in Yunan Province. This is geographically located a very long way from Beijing. The situation is that you have signed the joint venture agreement with the company in Beijing. This company with whom you have the agreement with are under the impression they are the only people you are connected with in China.

To apply Strategy Twenty you '*do something unusually strange and unexpected*', which is to mention that you are also negotiating to open an early learning centre with another Chinese company in Kunming. By applying Strategy Twenty you show your partners in Beijing that you are not limited to them as your only business partnership.

Negotiating in a Western Environment

EXAMPLE FOUR
Enacting Strategy Twenty

You are a tax-consultant who helps businesses ensure they meet the legal requirements for their business when conducting business internationally. Many of your clients are experienced business people whose companies have done well in the domestic market and are looking to expand and sell their products to overseas customers. As you have been dealing with these businesses for a long time you know that many of these business owners would prefer to try to work out the tax requirements themselves and therefore do not want to pay your fees for this service.

To apply Strategy Twenty you '*create confusion to weaken their perception and judgement*' by structuring your services so that new clients can buy a 'do-it-yourself' package for international tax. For a low price you will source all the documents and forms that they are likely to require, ensuring that their business is compliant with international tax regulations. For your full fee you offer a comprehensive audit of a client's business to determine compliance and to help them to meet all the required regulations.

When you meet with a potential new client and sense that they are reluctant to take up the full service that you offer, you tell them that it is common for business owners to want to take care of this for themselves, although they are often unsure where to start. You inform them you can provide them with a 'do-it-yourself' package that includes all the documents and forms they will need. In most cases the client is likely to sign up for this deal.

However, the 'do-it-yourself' package is not tailored to the client's specific business, which means it includes all documents the customer may need and also some that they may not need. Clients quickly realise the complexity of the task and often will struggle to determine what is relevant to their business and what is not, and become perplexed by the legal jargon and unfamiliar procedures. To take advantage of your client's '*disrupted thinking*' you call them in the week following the delivery of the documents to see how they are going. Usually your client will tell you that they cannot make sense of the documents and ask for your help. You are more than happy to sign them up for your full service and in this way you have successfully applied Strategy Twenty.

Key Points when using Strategy Twenty
- Most Chinese business people are prepared to negotiate in business and will appreciate a foreign business partner who is willing to do the same.
- When in negotiations with a potential Chinese business partner, take control and tell them your partnership will not be an exclusive agreement.
- When offering a service, give potential clients a taste of what you can provide, creating the desire to use your services regardless of the cost.

Shed your skin like the golden cicada -
means "to create a distraction that allows you to withdraw unnoticed"

When you are in danger of being defeated, and your only chance is to escape and regroup, then create an illusion. While the enemy's attention is focused on this artifice, secretly remove your men, leaving behind only a façade of your presence.

D uring the West Han era in China, Xiang Yu, who was the leader of Chu, prepared and guided his army to attack Liu Bang, who was the Han Emperor. He cleverly cornered Liu Ban in the fortified city of Xing Yang. Liu Bang's army were quickly running low on food and other necessary supplies. They were aware that if they did not escape, they would not survive. For Liu Bang's army there were only two ways out of this situation. One way was to surrender and be defeated by Xiang Xu's army and the other way was to starve to death. Neither of these options were desirable. Xiang Yu knew that once the Liu Bang army had become weakened from lack of food and water they would be easy to defeat. One of Liu Bang's generals, known to be an expert strategist, applied Strategy

Twenty-One – **Shed your skin like a golden cicada** to the situation. Liu Bang's men were '*in danger of being defeated, and their only chance was to escape and regroup, then create an illusion*'. To enable them to escape, Liu Bang's strategist had 2,000 women dressed as armoured soldiers. Just before the light of dawn the 2,000 women, now looking like the Liu Bang army of men, stood in front of the western gate of the city in battle formation. In the middle of this formation was the strategist general disguised as Emperor Liu Bang. He gave the signal for surrender, which presented the illusion that the Emperor and his army were surrendering. They displayed in front of the Xiang Yu army that the reason for this surrender was because they had run out of food, which seemed feasible. This made the soldiers of Xiang Yu feel they had beaten the Liu Bang army. This impression was created because '*their attention was focused on the artifice*'. While this illusion was going on, Liu Bang quietly escaped from the fortified city and '*secretly removed some of his men*' through the east gate of Xing Yang, '*leaving behind only a façade of his presence*', which was the general pretending to be him.

Xiang Yu realised he had been tricked, and was so furious he had the general who was pretending to be Emperor Liu Bang burned to death. The general's sacrifice was worthwhile, because Emperor Liu Bang of West Han was saved. Therefore, the end result was that Strategy Twenty-One was successfully applied.

When Strategy Twenty-One is used, the strategist creates a distraction so that the person or people involved can withdraw unnoticed from a difficult situation. The main skill in applying Strategy Twenty-One is to understand what is most important. In this situation, even though the general who applied the strategy was killed, the emperor was able to escape and was therefore saved, which was the main goal of the application of Strategy Twenty-One.

Strategy Twenty-One may look like Strategy Six – **Make a noise in the east and attack in the west** from Book One – *Tame the Tiger: Negotiating from a position of power*, however, the difference is that Strategy Six is about shifting attention, whereas Strategy Twenty-One is about creating a façade. Strategy Twenty-One can also look like Strategy Seventeen – **Toss out a brick to attract jade** from Book Three – *Lure the Tiger: Negotiation in confronting circumstances*, although the difference is that Strategy Seventeen is about giving up something to receive something of greater value, as opposed to creating a façade to retain what you have.

Negotiating with Chinese People

Example One
Strategy Twenty-One in action (against you)

One of the Chinese communication behaviours that Western people often find difficult to comprehend is when a Chinese businessperson says 'yes' when they really mean 'no'. Using this style of communication may be a way of applying Strategy Twenty-One.

In this scenario you are a business that produces high-quality beef in your home country, and you are planning to export your beef to China. You are visiting China for the first time. Over the last year you have heard from several sources that high-quality beef is a sought-after product in China. This news has encouraged you to put the resources in place to export your product to China. You have contacted your in-country representatives and they have organised several meetings for you with Chinese distributors in China. All of these distributors are well connected and have strong *guanxi* with many upmarket supermarkets in China. The city you have been advised to focus on is Qingdao in Shandong Province. Shandong Province is not as saturated with Western products as are other bigger cities, and people in Qingdao are very interested in being introduced to high-quality Western products, so you believe this a good option. Out of the five companies you meet with to distribute your product, you decide to focus on one particular distributor. This is because they have clearly conveyed to you that they can get your products into reputable supermarkets. You return to your own country feeling confident about your decision. While all of this is going on your chosen distributor is also talking with your competitors about exporting their beef products into China. During your discussions with your chosen distributor you shared a lot of information, such as pricing and suggested packaging. Throughout your communications your selected distributor has continued to say 'yes' they are interested in dealing with you, when they actually mean 'no'. They have been applying Strategy Ten – **Hide your dagger behind a smile** from Book Two – *Deceive the Dragon: Negotiating to retain power*. Saying 'yes' when they really mean 'no' enables them to continue to develop *guanxi* with you. This provides a base for the successful application of Strategy Twenty-One. Even though you are aware that the company you have chosen to deal with has been experiencing some financial difficulties, you are not concerned by this information as you see them as an honest company. You visited their office in Qingdao, and everything seemed to be working efficiently. They have also offered you a very good deal. Therefore there are several reasons as to why you have decided to focus on them. What you do not realise is '*they are in danger and their only chance is to escape and regroup*', and to do so '*they create an illusion*'. Your attention has been focused on the many opportunities they have discussed, and you do not realise these opportunities are not real, because '*your attention is focused on this artifice*'.

Now you have selected this distributor, you return to your own country to organise all of the logistics to export your high-quality beef to Qingdao. Over the next few months you work on setting up everything in your business, which includes getting packaging and freight documentation in order, before beginning the shipping process. On your return to China your beautifully packaged beef is set to arrive in the port of Qingdao. When you arrived you found it odd that your distributors did not offer to pick you up from the airport. They also did not meet you at the hotel or host you for dinner, which you found strange. When you went to their office there was just the sign of the company on the door and the whole office had been vacated. '*They secretly removed everything leaving behind only a façade of their presence'.* Meanwhile, from your conversations with this company, they now have a lot of information about the meat industry. You have a shipment arriving any day and you attend a networking function to find out that your distributor is now dealing with another foreign beef producer. By saying 'yes' to you they have kept your focus on the deal while they have been communicating with a major competitor. You were so focused on the deal which turned out to be *'a façade'* you did not see that Strategy Twenty-One was being applied.

EXAMPLE ONE
Guarding yourself against Strategy Twenty-One

In this situation, to guard yourself against Strategy Twenty-One, a good idea would be to develop relationships with the other distributors you initially met. Choosing just one distributor limits your options with this potentially large export market and places you in a risky situation. Also, until a deal is definitely signed, it is not a good idea to share with the distributor all of the specific details of your industry. Of course, there are certain things you must disclose to move forward with the deal, however, do not disclose what you do not have to. When you are meeting with a potential distributor and they say 'yes', keep in mind this doesn't necessarily mean they are really interested in distributing your product. In Chinese business communication, 'yes' often doesn't mean 'yes'.

EXAMPLE TWO
Strategy Twenty-One in action (against you)

In a scenario where you are importing children's toys from a factory in Guangdong Province, which is in the south of China, you find yourself in a situation where Strategy Twenty-One has been applied on you. You have been dealing with a factory for five years and everything has been operating very smoothly. The quality of products is of a high standard, things are delivered on time, their prices are reasonable and the best thing is they communicate well in English so there is no language barrier. Your market is children aged from four to eight. The toys are very educational and consist of games and objects which children have to assemble, with strong learning outcomes. The purchasers of your products are parents, early learning centres, and primary schools. In this segment of the children's early learning toy market you have established a strong reputation as a supplier of high quality durable educational toys. This is largely because the toys are constructed from excellent materials. Your manufacturer also supplies excellent packaging for each individual product. As the factory you are dealing with always delivers what you require, you see no reason to source another manufacturer. You have often been advised by your colleagues that it is risky to only deal with one factory in China, because if something happens and you lose this connection you have no backup.

During the last six months your manufacturer in China has experienced some financial difficulties due to the increased costs of running their factory. You are unaware of this and have not observed anything unusual. Your products are delivered in the usual way, and when collected from the delivery location you only ever see the impressive outer packaging. Over the past six months you have had many customers complaining about the quality of your products. These complaints include your products not being as durable as they should be, which means that consumers are finding the toys easily break. During the time that your manufacturer has been experiencing financial difficulties, they have located another supplier of materials to construct the toys. Materials from this new supplier are less expensive. The result is that the products made with the materials provided by the new supplier are of a lower quality. However, your manufacturer has maintained the high-quality packaging so you are not aware of this change. In this way your supplier has applied Strategy Twenty-One. They '*created an illusion*' with the usual elaborate packaging '*leaving only a façade*' of the original product inside.

After the application of Strategy Twenty-One, you are in a position where you are dealing with a manufacturer supplying a lower-quality product. You have lost customers and are finding it difficult to recoup the profits you are losing. What was going well for five years has now taken a direction that is devastating for the toy business you have created.

EXAMPLE TWO
Guarding yourself against Strategy Twenty-One

To guard yourself against Strategy Twenty-One, it would be wise to establish relationships with more than one manufacturer in China. It is advised to deal with at least two or even three factories, in case one of the factories becomes difficult to deal with. Also, even though you are dealing with people who speak English, which is a bonus; this will not mean you will understand everything that is going on. Do not forget that there are wide cultural differences between Western and Chinese cultures. Listen carefully to what your home country business colleagues are saying, as they may have useful experiences to share with you. When your products arrive from China, do not just take for granted they will be the same product you always buy. Open a representative sample of items to see if the product inside is what you have paid for. The quality of packaging may not reflect the contents. Even if you feel extremely confident with the factory you are dealing with, the situation can change quickly and complacency will not help you keep abreast of what is going on. It is wise to take the extra time to routinely check that the desired quality has been maintained.

Key Points when Strategy Twenty-One is used against you

- When you hear 'yes' this can often mean 'no'.
- Do not rely solely on the packaging to judge the quality of your product.
- Even if your Chinese contacts speak English they will still conduct business in a Chinese manner.

EXAMPLE THREE
Enacting Strategy Twenty-One

It is very popular for Chinese people to visit Western countries and study business-focused topics for short periods of time. You own and operate an organisation, and annually for the last five years you have hosted a group of senior government officials from China to complete a five-day course in project management. This course is tailored for the Chinese group and you are providing high-level interpretation, as their government officials do not speak English. The course commences every year at the beginning of October, which is a good time for these officials because there is a week-long holiday in China starting from the 1st October. They experience a foreign culture, complete a five-day course in Western project management, and have some time for sightseeing. Your organisation runs this training to be cost-neutral, as it is through teaching these courses to influential people that you have built a strong *guanxi* with your most valuable Chinese contacts, which has led to other profitable business.

The usual itinerary is that the group arrive on a Sunday, and on the Sunday night you organise a welcome dinner. They are fully engaged in their course from Monday to Friday, and on the Friday night they have a graduation dinner and receive their certificates for the completion of the course. On the Saturday they are taken on a sightseeing tour, followed by a farewell dinner, and on Sunday they fly back to China.

You are now approaching the sixth year of the delivery of this course. It is January and, as you have done in previous years, you commence the preparation for your Chinese group to visit in October. The training venue that you have utilised for the last five years is in an upmarket function centre, in an excellent location, and has a high-level reputation in your city. You discover that the function centre has been sold and the new owners have increased the rent for the training room. Catering costs have also risen substantially. It will now not be viable for you to continue to use this venue because the cost incurred will be too high. However, you do not want to cancel the course because running these courses has been the key ingredient to developing your *guanxi*, which has led to other profitable business opportunities. To continue delivering the course you can apply Strategy Twenty-One, as you will have to '*regroup, and then create an illusion*'. You search your city and locate another venue at a reasonable price. This venue is not as upmarket as the previous location. Even so, by applying Strategy Twenty-One you can continue to uphold your reputation without losing money. To do that you invest in some large banners displaying your course and business details. You spend some extra money making your training materials look more stylish. Your Chinese participants' attention will be '*focused on the banners and materials*', and therefore they will not notice the lower-quality location. You have brought with you a '*façade of your presence*', which is the high-quality location. You have created an illusion by providing high-quality banners with colourful advertising and good quality training materials, and because your participants will be focused on these details they will not be aware they are in a lower-quality venue. In this way you have successfully applied Strategy Twenty-One.

Negotiating in a Western Environment

Example Four
Enacting Strategy Twenty-One

Imagine you run a store that sells air conditioners and space heaters. In addition to having a showroom and several sales staff you also employ people to do the installation and maintenance. In recent years, while there was a lot of new construction in the areas near your shop, you sold a lot of products. However, as construction in the area has slowed so have your sales. You consider closing your store. After weighing up your options, you decide to keep the store open and implement Strategy Twenty-One. You decide to increase the number of employees working in your installation and maintenance department and shift the focus of your business from sales to maintenance. Instead of concentrating on selling and installing new units, you concentrate on building up the maintenance work. You approach one of the suppliers from whom you buy the air-conditioner units and negotiate to provide maintenance for their units even if you did not sell or install them. When people see your company vehicles out on the road going from job to job and associate the company branding with your shop they assume that you must be doing a lot of new installations.

You have applied Strategy Twenty-One by *'regrouping, and then creating an illusion'*. Once this idea is well established, you are able to heavily reduce the size of your showroom and the number of employees working in the sales department. The shop is left behind, and you have *'secretly moved the focus of your businesses'* from sales to mobile repairs.

Key Points when using Strategy Twenty-One

- When changing the quality of your product create a distraction so it goes unnoticed.
- Invest in things that you can control to mask the things you cannot.
- Save 'face' by creating the illusion that you are something that you are not.

Shut the door to catch the thief *means* "*lock them in to retain your power*"

If you have the chance to completely capture the enemy, then you should do so, thereby bringing the battle or war to a quick and lasting conclusion. To allow the enemy to escape plants the seeds of future conflict. But if they succeed in escaping, be wary of giving chase.

*J*n China's Tang Dynasty, during the reign of Empress Wu Ze Tian, there were two ministers who were favoured by her, and their job was to devise torture instruments. Their names were Lai Jun Chen and Jhou Sing. Criminals who were tortured using the instruments these two ministers designed experienced so much suffering that the pain they endured would quickly send them to the point of confession. Empress Wu Ze Tian received information from a reliable source that Jhou Sing was plotting a revolt against her power. The empress talked with Lai Jun Chen about this situation and ordered him to find out how Jhou Sing was planning this revolt against her. Once he had gained this knowledge, Lai Jun Chen was then ordered to arrest Jhou Sing. To successfully accomplish this task Lai Jun Chen applied Strategy Twenty-Two – **Shut the door to catch the thief** on Jhou Sing. His plan was to set a situation up so he would have the chance to '*completely capture*' Jhou

Sing, and therefore '*bring the situation to a quick and lasting conclusion*'. If he '*allowed Jhou Sing to escape this would plant the seed for future conflict*'. This was quite a difficult task for Lai Jun Chen because he was aware of Jhou Sing's excellent torture techniques, and therefore it would be hard to perform a torture technique on Jhou Sing to make him confess to this planned revolt against the empress. To apply Strategy Twenty-Two he invited Jhou Sing to eat a meal with him, and he told Jhou Sing he needed his help to solve a problem. Lai Jun Chen explained to Jhou Sing that he felt that criminals were becoming more resistant to torture techniques and they were refusing to confess even under the harshest of conditions. He was seeking advice from Jhou Sing to see if he had any other torture techniques that would push people to confess. Jhou Sing shared with Lai Jun Chen that an excellent torture technique was to use a large jar, big enough to fit a person, filled with boiling water. The suspect would be immersed in this boiling water if they did not confess. They would often confess straight away, and if they didn't confess straight away they would be put into this boiling water and soon after they would confess. After Jhou Sing had shared this torture technique, Lai Jun Chen expressed how disgusted he was that Jhou Sing had a plot planned against Empress Wu Zu Tian. He said that the empress was aware of this plot and had ordered him to investigate Jhou Sing. He ordered Jhou Sing to confess, and stated that if he did not confess he would have him forced into the jar of boiling water. Lai Jun Chen had successfully applied Strategy Twenty-Two because Jhou Sing confessed his plot against the empress.

Strategy Twenty-Two requires the strategist to conduct some detailed research. When Strategy Twenty-Two is applied the initial offer may seem very good. However, all possible outcomes of the deal need to be considered.

Negotiating with Chinese People

EXAMPLE ONE
Strategy Twenty-Two in action (against you)

You are planning to export your high-quality cheese to China. You have heard cheese is fast becoming a popular consumable in China. You have also attended several export presentations in your home country which have discussed the popularity of your product in China and validated your future export plans. China is a new place for you to export your products. Knowing that it is a very different culture, you decide to hire a space in a food exhibition to introduce your products. This exposure gives you an understanding of the Chinese market. At the exhibition you have diligently organised samples of your cheeses and also hired an experienced interpreter. Everything over the two days of the trade show goes very well. You have many people tasting your cheeses and the interpreter is doing a good job of explaining the different varieties, the geographical locations they are from, and the etiquette that goes with eating cheese. During the exhibition you meet a company you perceive to be an excellent distributor. You base your judgement on the fact that they have solid *guanxi* in many of the upmarket supermarkets in Shanghai, Beijing, and Qingdao. They also have a team of people who speak very good English, and because you do not speak or understand Mandarin Chinese, this makes your situation much easier.

You have been in the business of making cheese for over three decades, and in the last five years you have developed a unique piece of technology, which is an automated system to produce your boutique product.

The distributor you meet at the exhibition is very interested in marketing your product, because of the quality and the uniqueness of how the product is made. This kind of product will give your distributor 'face' to their clients. Your distributor is able to negotiate with the supermarkets they are connected with to give you free space to set up tasting samples. They say the time frame for this deal is unknown, but this is not an issue as the supermarkets are very interested in your cheeses. During the year following the exhibition things seem to be going very well. In the second year some of the distribution team allude to wanting to visit your country to see how your cheese production technology works. In order to develop *guanxi* you not only invite two people to your country, you also pay for their travel costs. They stay in your country for five days and spend each day in your cheese factory. They are given the chance to completely understand the technology. In your opinion this is a good idea because the more they understand about your product the easier it will be for them to market it in China. You have not asked them to sign a confidentiality agreement because you perceive them as trustworthy.

After two years of dealing with this Chinese distributor

they inform you that the main supermarket chain you are dealing with now needs to charge for the space to offer samples inside the supermarkets. To cover these new expenses you need to increase your product prices. After this increase in price your distributor reduces their imports of your products. The people at the distribution company are also aware of how your technology works because of the time they spent in your factory. They use their new knowledge of cheese to look for other cheese exporters with whom they share your unique technology to significantly reduce labour costs. From this application of Strategy Twenty-Two you will quickly reach a conclusion that your current export strategy is not profitable. It will be difficult for you to rebuild your China business because you have only dealt with one distributor and have not built up any *guanxi* with other distributors. What seemed like a perfect situation has resulted in another company using something very similar to your technology.

The Chinese distributor has been able to slightly modify your technology so it is not exactly the same, and they are still staying within the boundaries of the intellectual property laws. They have successfully applied Strategy Twenty-Two.

EXAMPLE ONE
Guarding yourself against Strategy Twenty-Two

In this situation there was not enough research conducted. Just one trade show was not adequate research and experience of the Chinese market to make a judgement about who to work with. Using only one distributor in

China is very risky because if things change, there are no alternatives. When you are in the position of needing distribution in China it is advisable to use at least two or three different distributors. This structure also creates a situation where the distributors will be in competition with one another, and will be more likely to give you high-quality service and a good deal. The fact that the distributor's staff have good English is also not a good enough reason to decide on any one distributor. Relying on their English places you in a dependent position, and gives the distributor additional power. In this case it would have been wise to employ at least one Mandarin speaker. Then the distributor would perceive you as having more cultural resources. While it was a great idea to invite the distributors' staff to the cheese factory to educate them, the five day visit was too long, as it enabled them to learn too much about your unique technology.

A signed confidentiality agreement, presented in both English and Chinese, should have been required before they viewed your unique technology. When asking Chinese people to sign an agreement it is important to ask them what the confidentiality agreement means to them. You may find that what such an agreement means to you may be different to what it means to your Chinese contact. To read the words is only one step. Getting the person to explain back to you what it means will show you their understanding of the conditions of the agreement.

When visiting China with the aim of discussing issues such as price it is highly unlikely you will be able to get your Chinese contacts to sit down and talk with you directly. It is likely that they will steer the conversation away from your main topic and onto other potentially unrelated matters.

Instead of agreeing with everything the distributor advises you to do, push back and show you are in charge, and not a subordinate willing to simply accommodate all of their ideas. Constructing the intellectual property in such a way that it cannot be duplicated easily would have been a good business decision from the beginning. Given the uniqueness of your method and the risk of it being copied, you could have considered licencing your intellectual property, because in this way you would get an ongoing fee. A strategy may be to give your distributor the task of selling licences, which would give them a sense of ownership.

When something is offered free of charge, such as free space inside supermarkets to distribute samples of your product, it is probable that such a situation will not go on indefinitely. There should have been a plan in place for when the supermarkets begin to charge a fee. In this situation many things were not considered, so it was easy for the distributor to successfully apply Strategy Twenty-Two.

EXAMPLE TWO
Strategy Twenty-Two in action (against you)

The trend in China is toward older people in their retirement wanting to live in a retirement village. In traditional culture, when people retired, they looked after their grandchildren. However, with smaller families and many parents sending their children to childcare there is not as much need for grandparents' help. The strong economy means that China's large middle-class population also have more money to spend for their retirement years to reside in communities of similar aged people.

Your area of business is in the development and management of retirement villages. You explore this opportunity by visiting China, and your in-country government office has organised several meetings for you with possible business partners and companies interested in building retirement villages. On your trip to China you show potential partners photographs of the retirement villages you have built and now manage in your country. You have three decades of experience in this industry, which is impressive to Chinese business people. One company in particular shows enormous interest in your company, and requests to visit your country to see your work firsthand. After visiting five of your retirement villages they are very keen to work with you. They want you to sign a contract for the development of a retirement village project to be finished in China within three years. The contract requires that two of your experienced team will travel to China four times a year for the next three years. They would like your consulting fees to be at a slightly lower price in exchange for 10% of the retirement village business when it is operational. At the beginning of the project this seems like a very good deal, and you agree to their requests and start the project. You were not aware that from the time you were introduced to them they were planning to sell the completed retirement village. To have this plan in place may be unusual business behaviour to a Western business person. However, for a Chinese business person this is something that is quite normal. Such practice is explained by Strategy Twelve – **Seize the opportunity to lead a sheep away** in Book Two: *Deceive the Dragon: Negotiating to retain power*, which is about continually searching for opportunities. The fact that they are looking for someone to purchase the retirement village is something they will have decided before beginning the negotiation process with you. At the end of the three years you are expecting to own 10% of the completed retirement village. Six months before completion the company you are working for locates a buyer for the village. Over the last few years they have applied Strategy Twenty-Two and have given themselves '*the chance to completely capture you*', because the new owners are only willing to give you 5% of the completed village rather than the 10% you had originally negotiated. You had no idea that this retirement village in China would be sold and you were looking forward to getting 10% of the village at the end of the project. However, if you received 10% then the original owners would not have been able to sell the village, so they told the buyers that your share would be 5%. There was nothing written into the contract that states new owners must continue with the original deal which gives you 10%, because you never expected the village to be sold. In this case, Strategy Twenty-Two has been successfully applied because you have given your consulting services to the company for a lower price, thinking that in three years you would have 10% of the business. You are now left with only 5%, which certainly does not give you adequate remuneration for your work. For you, this has resulted in a '*quick and lasting conclusion*', leaving you with an unsatisfactory financial result. Although you have gained enormous experience in the Chinese market, it has come at a considerable cost.

Example Two
Guarding yourself against Strategy Twenty-Two

To guard yourself against Strategy Twenty-Two it would have been beneficial to consider when signing a contract which extends over a three-year period that during this time things can change dramatically. China has a rapidly evolving business culture, and entrepreneurs are continually considering new ventures and are likely to change directions quickly.

It would have been a more useful approach to consider right from the outset the risk you ran of not receiving the 10% that was being offered to you. If you had acknowledged that you may not receive the 10% once the project was complete, then you could have considered what you would do in that circumstance. For example, you might have asked your Chinese company to pay for your travelling and other expenses during the three-year period, as an alternative or an addition to the 10% offer. As the skills you and your team possess are highly sought-after, and because this sector is in high demand in China, the consulting fees could have been higher to cover the cost, even if you only received 5%

of the completed project. Research the demand for your product in China, and also your competition. Once you have an accurate view of the situation you may well be able to negotiate a higher fee.

Key Points when Strategy Twenty-Two is used against you

- It is important to consider using multiple distributors to fall back on if something goes wrong.
- Ensure your distributors sign a confidentiality agreement that is written in both English and Chinese, to ensure shared understanding.
- Do not give your distributors the chance to completely understand your technology.

EXAMPLE THREE
Enacting Strategy Twenty-Two

Strategy Twenty-Two is a very clever strategy for you to apply on Chinese business people, because the successful application of this strategy gives you a lot more control. Often, when you are not from China, setting up a partnership with Chinese business people or dealing with a Chinese distributor means you have to rely on their *guanxi*. Relying on your Chinese business partner or distributor's *guanxi* leaves you with limited resources, because a major resource is your *guanxi*.

Take a situation where you are a wine company, and the distributor with whom you have been dealing for the past three years has suggested you set up a cellar door in

Qingdao, which is a large port city in Shandong Province. The population of Shandong is very interested in learning more about wines, as Shandong Province is well known for its beer, known as Qingdao beer, so they are very familiar with being the province in China renowned for its alcohol. Opening a cellar door requires a lot of organisation with things such as location and fitting, and a selection of influential people to invite to taste your wine at the opening. To apply Strategy Twenty-Two successfully, from the time that you decided you will go forward with this plan you need to attend all meetings that have any relevance for this cellar door's venture. The idea is for you to develop as much *guanxi* as possible so you '*have the chance to completely capture these important connections*'. If you do not speak Mandarin, hire an experienced interpreter to accompany you to these meetings, even if the officials you meet speak English, so you have a better understanding of what is really going on by hiring an experienced interpreter. At these meetings do not rely on your distributor's interpreter. By developing as much *guanxi* as you can you will be much more independent. To develop this *guanxi* go to as many networking functions as possible. There are always numerous networking functions in China, and even if they do not seem relevant to your product you can put Strategy Twelve into action. So if you meet a Chinese business person who is not in your industry at a networking function, they are likely to have connections in your industry. In this way you can build your *guanxi* networks. When applying Strategy Twenty-Two you need to build your connections within your distributor's networks, and also independently of your distributor. Once you have these connections solidly built you will have more control. Should a situation arise where you do not want to continue doing business with this distributor, you will be able to locate another distributor who meets your requirements without too much damage to your business in China. At some point you may feel that your distributor is taking too much profit and the successful application of Strategy Twenty-Two gives you the freedom to search for another distributor and not be locked into a business situation that is no longer working well for you

Negotiating in a Western Environment

EXAMPLE FOUR
Enacting Strategy Twenty-Two

You run a clothing store. You hire several sales assistants. You notice one of your employees makes more sales than any of the others, and has a real talent for building relationships with customers. They are enthusiastic and help customers to feel good when they try on clothes, so customers trust them when they suggest additional items to purchase. You are concerned that this employee could be hired elsewhere and that you would lose someone who is very valuable to your business. You know you need to create the opportunity to '*completely capture them*' because your staff member has good sales skills, and so there is the possibility that they could make more money in a position that gives them more commission than you could match. To have a '*lasting conclusion*' you consider how you can retain them as a staff member without increasing their salary to a level that is unwise for your business. You decide that you will be able to retain this employee if you provide them with opportunities to advance in the business. You offer to sponsor them to do a long management course while they continue working for you. By doing so you have discouraged them from looking for other jobs that may not give them opportunities like this. You have also incentivised them to stay because they will not be able to finish the course if they go to another employer.

Key Points when using Strategy Twenty-Two

- Develop as much *guanxi* with Chinese business people as possible in order to retain control of your product.
- Complete your research and understand the market you are engaging in.
- Offer something that the recipient cannot receive from another source.

Befriend a distant enemy to attack one nearby *means "build alliances with businesses across related industries"*

It is known that nations that border each other become enemies, while nations separated by distance and obstacles make better allies. When you are the strongest in one field, your greatest threat comes from the second strongest in your field, not the strongest from another field.

*I*n ancient China, Henan Province had endured extreme droughts and floods which left the province in a devastating situation. This situation was particularly bad for the population because the harvests had been poor, and so the people starved. There was no hope of getting any outside relief because there were many bandits and robbers who roamed around terrorising the population. Yu Hu, who was a high-level provincial officer, was appointed by the Henan provincial government to try to restore some order in the province. He had the reputation of being a very clever strategist, and he decided to apply Strategy Twenty-Three - **Befriend a distant enemy to attack one nearby** to resolve this situation and bring order to the people of Henan Province. To apply Strategy Twenty-Three he announced that he was going to organise a military force and that he was in search of recruits. His first move towards finding these recruits was to issue a pardon to people who had committed crimes if they joined his military force. This meant if they joined up with him, they would no longer be prosecuted for their past crimes. He cleverly organised three classes of troops. The first class consisted of men who had committed robbery and murder. The second class consisted of men who had committed theft. The third class were men who had joined groups that had chosen to be robbers or thieves mostly because they wanted to avoid normal everyday labour. Within a month Yu Hu had over three hundred recruits. He paraded these troops before him, announcing that their past crimes would be forgiven and that they would be free of being prosecuted. They stood tall in their army uniforms, which made them feel like worthy citizens as opposed to their usual criminal identity. This gave them 'face'.

Yu Hu was *separated from these criminals by having a very different history*' and for this reason they *made better allies*'. To have their past misdeeds forgiven, they had to do something for Henan Province. This task was to find all of their criminal colleagues who had not answered Yu Hu's call to join his military force. He cleverly paid the first two classes of men the highest salaries because he knew they were the more strategic criminals and would know many of the bandits who were disrupting Henan Province. This task took them one year, and resulted in the province becoming safe.

Strategy Twenty-Three enables the strategist to create an alliance with someone who is distant from them. In Yu Hu's situation he created an alliance with the criminals. These criminals were able to do the work that was difficult for him to do because people with past criminal histories would be far more likely to know how to find active criminals.

When Strategy Twenty-Three is used, the strategist creates a well thought through alliance that is distant from them in values or products and services. They use this alliance to achieve a task and therefore get what they want. Yu Hu used his military forces, who were former criminals, to eliminate the criminals currently plaguing the country. He offered them a clean record if they located the criminals who were terrorising Henan province. He was a very clever strategist because he paid the criminals with a history of committing serious crimes the highest price to join this brigade. He did this because he knew they would be the group closest to other criminals who were terrorising Henan Province. Strategy Twenty-Three is about making the right alliances to achieve the best outcomes.

Negotiating with Chinese People

EXAMPLE ONE
Strategy Twenty-Three in action (against you)

You run an early childhood learning centre, and are well-established with a good reputation in your own country. Your interest in the Chinese market became ignited when you attended an export seminar in your country where you became aware of the popularity of early childhood learning. Chinese parents have become concerned about their children's future and want them to be as well-educated as possible, which includes learning English from a young age. You decide it would be an excellent idea to export your early childhood learning curriculum to China. Your curriculum focuses on the 0-6 age group. You had been advised to hire a booth inside an early childhood learning exhibition in China, and you visit three cities on three different occasions, using this introduction method. These cities are Guangzhou, Chengdu, and Shanghai. You feel you and your team have learnt a lot at these exhibitions. Your observation at these exhibitions was that people were only mildly interested, which you thought strange, because you assumed interest would have been higher, considering you had been informed that early childhood education was fast becoming an educational product in high demand in China.

At these exhibitions the Chinese childcare providers who approached you were friendly and gave you great acknowledgement for your product, but that is where the interest in your services appeared to stop. They seemed more interested in other stands at the exhibitions that sold toys and early childhood learning equipment instead. You decided to go over to the toys section with your interpreter and introduce yourself, seeing them also as prospective clients. You discussed the lowering of your prices to gain some positive responses and were able to achieve invitations to meet early learning centres that are clients of these equipment sellers. Your immediate thought was that your price was too high, because after lowering the prices you were invited to their centres. What you did not realise was that at that time the early learning centres in China did not have a curriculum for the 0-3 age group. At the exhibitions you were the only foreign company that had a high-quality 0-3 early childcare curriculum. The early learning centres applied Strategy Twenty-Three on you, because you had to pursue them and lower your price to gain any interest. The early learning centres were the '*strongest in their field*' and they aligned themselves at the exhibition with the '*strongest in another field*', which were the toys and early learning equipment representatives. This interest in another area at the exhibition encouraged you to connect with them and to pursue them at the exhibition. When you eventually signed deals with childcare centres in each city for a lower price, you did not realise until the completion of the deal that what you had was a highly sought-after early learning product. You thought they were interested in the whole 0-6 program, and you were in a competitive market. However, your 0-3 information was all they really wanted. There were very few people in the market that had this product.

The early learning centres applied Strategy Twenty-Three by encouraging you to approach them via another component of the industry, which was not the same as the childcare centre. Their apparent interest in another companies' products drove you to pursue them, and in doing so you lowered the price because you did not realise you had a sought-after product.

EXAMPLE ONE
EXAMPLE ONE
Guarding yourself against Strategy Twenty-Three

In this situation, to guard yourself against Strategy Twenty-Three, it would have been wise to gain more information from the seminar you attended in your own country. Finding out more specific information, such as what age group the early childcare centres in China were interested in would have been extremely beneficial. You assumed there would be interest in a curriculum for the 0-6 age group. If you had known that the real interest was for the 0-3 age group and that you had a sought-after product then you may not have been so willing to pursue these potential customers at the exhibition and to lower your price. Besides, there are other ways to enter the Chinese market beyond participation in exhibitions, such as going to networking events or attending tradeshows and simply being an observer. When Strategy Twenty-Three was applied you assumed there was little interest in your product and that you had a lot of competitors, not realising you were one of the few foreign early learning centres that had a reputable 0-3 age group curriculum to take to China. When the potential customers aligned themselves with other companies who were not the same as them this prompted you to talk with them by going over to the stand and introducing yourself. In this scenario the main issue was insufficient research into what the market really wanted. If you had gained more information this would have given you confidence. You could have applied Strategy Nine – **Watching the fire on the opposite shore** from Book

Two: *Negotiating to retain power*, and just waited for them to come back to you because you have a product they wanted, and you did not need to lower your price. Applying Strategy Twenty-Three would have then been unsuccessful.

EXAMPLE TWO
Strategy Twenty-Three in action (against you)

A scenario may be that you are an architectural company who has successfully been dealing with a large design company in China for five years. Things have been going smoothly and you have dealt with every challenge. The design company in China likes dealing with you because you deliver on time, and you deliver a high-quality unique product. Your company has won awards both in your home country and internationally. Therefore, dealing with your company has given your Chinese client 'face'. Your company specialises in the design of hotels and large commercial offices. Over these five years you have also had requests to design hospitals, schools, retirement facilities, and childcare centres. When these proposals are put forward, because your company has specialised skills only in certain areas, you bring in other design companies who have the skills you need to complete these proposals. You have always maintained control of the proposal and guarded yourself against Strategy Six – **Make a noise in the east and attack in the west** from Book One: Tame the Tiger: *Negotiating from a position of power*, which is where you may be diverted away from the main point. Over the five years you have been working with the design company in China. You have completed projects for two large office buildings, a hotel, a hospital, a retirement village with one hundred units, and a primary school for international students.

You are transparent with the Chinese company. While your proposal says that the project will be fully managed by your company, you list all the other companies that you plan to work with. The companies that you use do not have the same skills as you, making you '*the strongest in one field, and your greatest threat is the second strongest in your field*'.

In this way you inform the Chinese company who you are working with. With the information you provide they no longer need you to handle the whole architectural design, and can approach the companies that are '*the second strongest in your field*' directly for projects that are not in your area of expertise, such as hotels and commercial offices. Through the application of Strategy Twenty-Three you are no longer needed to complete all the architectural design projects that come across their desk, and are only called on when your particular skills are required.

Example Two
Guarding yourself against Strategy Twenty-Three

To guard yourself against Strategy Twenty-Three in this situation, remember that when things are going smoothly it is important not to be complacent. Bringing other design companies in so that you can offer all the skills required to pitch for a large project is a great idea. However, too much transparency can be dangerous. By writing a proposal that openly displays the details of the other companies you are bringing in for the job you provide your Chinese clients with the perfect avenue to apply Strategy Twenty-Three on you.

The Chinese company may approach you to complete a very large project, aware you cannot do it alone. When approaching you in this way they are applying Strategy Thirteen – **Beat the grass to startle the snake** which is explained in Book Three – *Lure the Tiger: Negotiating in confronting circumstances.* By applying this strategy your Chinese client is trying to create a disruption, knowing that you probably do not have the resources. The best reaction is to calmly confirm that your company can do the project. You may only be able to complete the project by bringing in all of your contacts; however, you can present your proposal so that it looks as though your company is completing the whole project by itself. In this way you leave no opportunity for the Chinese company to contact the companies you are bringing in for the project. This will guard you against Strategy Twenty-Three.

Key Points when Strategy Twenty-Three is used against you

- Before commencing business in the Chinese market, research Chinese consumer needs thoroughly. If your product is in high demand you may be able to charge a higher price than you originally had in mind.
- When bringing in other companies to support you in a project that you lead, do not disclose their details, as this gives your Chinese client the opportunity to contact them directly.
- Do not become complacent, as your Chinese business partner will be looking for ways to achieve a more cost-effective deal.

Example Three
Enacting Strategy Twenty-Three

In this scenario you export premium honey to China from your home country. You have been doing this successfully for three years, and the success of this export business is the result of your application of Strategy Twenty-Three. The business model to keep your product constantly exporting into China is to have the appropriate distribution channels. This means that your distributors are allies as opposed to competitors. In the business of exporting honey '*you are the strongest business in your field, and you are aware that your greatest threat is the second strongest in your field, not the strongest from another field*'. You have three distributors you work with who send your products to different cities across China. Each of these distributors is based in a different location. The three distributors you work with all deal with products that have honey in their product range. One distributor works in Chengdu, which is in the west of China, and deals with health food products, and high-quality honey is considered to be an important part of their range. Another distributor deals with products such as premium olives and other boutique foods, and your honey also fits perfectly into their range. This company has distribution channels in Guangzhou, which is in the south of China. The third distributor imports dietary supplements such as fish oil and magnesium. In this distributor's network honey is regarded as a dietary supplement. This third distributor works in Qingdao, which is in the north-east of China.

These distributors are separated by product range and therefore make better allies, as opposed to competitors. The way that these connections have been strategically chosen, both in location and product range, means that by applying Strategy Twenty-Three you have provided a safeguard for yourself, because if things do not work out with one of these three distributors it will be easy for you to stop dealing with them, without much likelihood of it damaging your relationship with the other two distributors, because they do not deal in the same range of products

Negotiating in a Western Environment

EXAMPLE FOUR
Enacting Strategy Twenty-Three

Imagine that you work for a large company that sells safety equipment to other businesses. You manage an outlet but hope to move up to the regional manager position when your boss retires. You know that some of your colleagues who do the same job as you do at other outlets in your region are also interested in the job. You are *'the strongest in your field'*, and you are aware *'your greatest threat comes from the second strongest in your field, not the strongest from another field.'*

In the past you have worked hard to make a good impression on your boss and this has worked to your advantage. However, you know that some of the other outlet managers in your region also do the same. Although a recommendation from your boss after retirement will be valuable to you, you are concerned that you could get stuck in a very draining rivalry with your peers that could take up a lot of time and effort but still have an uncertain outcome.

In the time leading up to your boss's retirement you decide to concentrate your efforts on building relationships with outlet managers in other regions. You make time to meet with some of the outlet managers from other regions where you can share ideas and advice. While building these relationships you build up your reputation as someone who is helpful and proactive, and whom the regional outlet managers like to work with. You also look for opportunities to collaborate with these people on projects, and as a result you also make a good impression on their bosses, who are the managers of the other regions.

Your strategic networking decisions mean that you have come to know the managers of the other regions and have built a good reputation with them. When it comes to your boss's retirement and the selection of a replacement for their job your application is successful, because it is supported by the managers of the other regions who will become your peers.

Key Points when using Strategy Twenty-Three
- When looking for distributors to import your product, select at least three from different locations across China.
- Retain your power by selecting distributors who work with different types of products, even if they operate in the same industry sector.
- Be proactive in building the right alliances to achieve your desired outcomes.

Borrow the road to conquer Guo *means "when you are unable to succeed alone, engage in strategic partnerships to help you achieve your goals"*

Borrow the resources of an ally to attack a common enemy. Once the enemy is defeated use those resources to turn on the ally who lent them to you in first place.

*I*n the east of ancient China there were two small neighbouring states, which were known as Yu and Guo. These small states bordered the large, powerful territory of Jin. The leader of Jin wanted to conquer these smaller states so that he could expand Jin's territory. To do this, the Jin leader applied Strategy Twenty-Four - **Borrow the road to conquer Guo**. The Jin leader knew that the Yu leader had the reputation of being corrupt, and would therefore be likely to accept a bribe of gifts in exchange for a clear pathway to the state of Guo. The Jin leader was an excellent strategist and knew how to use the pathway of the Yu territory to conquer Guo, and then to conquer Yu.

For the Jin army to apply Strategy Twenty-Four they would '*borrow the resources of the ally*'. Yu was not on friendly terms with Guo, and its leader was happy to accept the bribe and let the Jin army go through the pathway to conquer Guo. When the bribe was offered, the Yu leader's adviser warned him that accepting gifts was not a wise thing to do, because he believed there would be some kind of payback for the gifts. The gifts were wine and beautiful food, which the Jin leader knew the Yu leader would like. The adviser also said that even though the Yu state was not on friendly terms with Guo, if Guo was defeated it would leave the small state of Yu vulnerable because they would have no geographic protection against neighbouring states. The leader of Yu was so overwhelmed with the beautiful gifts that he did not listen to his adviser's warning.

After the Jin army successfully conquered Guo, on their way back through the Yu territory they conquered Yu '*using Guo's resources to turn on the ally who had given them a safe passage to Guo.*' This was exactly what the Yu adviser had predicted. Jin then occupied a large territory because through the successful application of Strategy Twenty-Four, it had conquered both Yu and Guo.

When Strategy Twenty-Four is used, the strategist will temporarily form an alliance in order to achieve a significant part of their goal. Once the initial goal is achieved, the strategist will then take advantage of the resources their ally has provided, and use their ally's resources against them.

Negotiating with Chinese People

EXAMPLE ONE
Strategy Twenty-Four in action (against you)

Imagine you are planning to set up a meat export business to China. Your meat is very high quality, and consists of beef, lamb, and pork products. You have a farm in your own country which specialises in high-quality beef. You source the high-quality lamb and pork from two other speciality farms with whom you have been connected for many years. To explore the Chinese market you join a government delegation from your home country to visit China. On this trip you discover that Chinese people are very interested in high-quality meats. You meet with several distributors who displayed interest in your products. You were advised to use more than one distributor, because if you only use one distributor this places in you in risky position. The risk is where the distributor could go out of business or change management. You choose three distributors to distribute your products, and they are all in different cities. These cities are Guangzhou, Shanghai, and Chengdu, so your distribution is well spread out across China, and will reach a diverse range of customers. You visit China on a second trip and meet with your three chosen distributors, and you also go to several networking functions. These functions are not focused on importing food products. In fact, one of the functions was a real estate networking function. You have learnt that Chinese business people practice the 36 Strategies and a commonly used strategy is Strategy Twelve - **Seize the opportunity to lead the sheep away** from Book Two: *Deceive the Dragon: Negotiating to retain power.* This is where Chinese people will look for opportunities not necessarily related to the industries they work in. In this case, real estate is not related to the importing of meat products. However, there is likely to be someone there interested in importing your products. At this networking function you meet someone who has good connections with some distributors interested in importing your high quality-meat.

So now you have three distributors in place ready to import your product, and a real estate agent who has excellent connections with some other distributors. You feel as though you are doing pretty well for your future business. The real estate businessperson has had a lot of experience buying and selling properties outside China and also speaks excellent English, which is useful as you speak no Mandarin Chinese. Prior to commencing this import business your real estate contact wants to visit your home country to see the products they will be introducing to their distributor. None of the other distributors are interested in visiting your home country. They will import the products without visiting, as they feel they have enough information to get started. You felt it was slightly unusual for the real estate contact to visit. When you tried to question the purpose of the visit, they applied Strategy Six – **Make a noise in the east and attack in the west** from Book One - *Tame the Tiger: Negotiating from a position of power.* This is where you never got a clear answer to your question. However, you accepted the situation and were pleased to see them visit. After a tour of your beef farm they are impressed, and want to visit the lamb and pork farms. You take them to these places and they are extremely impressed. They are also pleased to be introduced to the owners of the properties.

You were unaware that they '*borrowed your resources*', which were your connections with the lamb and pork farm owners, and they offered to buy these farms at prices that were too good to refuse. After this sale occurred you lost your connections with the lamb and pork farms, and the new owners were able to export directly to China without having to go through your business. You can now only export your beef, which is not a sustainable export business.

The Chinese real estate company, who are now the owners of the pork and lamb businesses, then offer you a good price for your business. They had '*used your resources*', which were your connections, to help them buy the lamb and pork farms, and then '*turned the situation around on you*', setting it up so that they could buy your business. They had successfully applied Strategy Twenty-Four because, once you sell, they will own the beef, lamb, and pork farms and can deal directly with their Chinese distributors.

EXAMPLE ONE
Guarding yourself against Strategy Twenty-Four

In this situation, choosing three distributors was a good idea because this was a risk management strategy. However, to guard against Strategy Twenty-Four it would have been wise to get the meat export business started with the three distributors, and have this established for at least one year, with some solid connections and income being generated, before having the real estate contact visit your country. As much as it is very proactive to go to other networking functions in China to meet people, it is also a good idea to proceed cautiously. You do not have to just go along with whatever your contact wants. Business in China is a game and it is quite acceptable to push back. To guard against Strategy Twenty-Four, researching the real estate company would have been wise. If they are a real estate company that has bought and sold property overseas, it is likely they will be experts in this industry, and may well be interested in the purchase of property.

Instead, when they eventually visit, you then have your own connections through your three distributors in China, which would make it more difficult for them to persuade the lamb and pork farms to sell their properties, because you would have established solid connections and sales in China. If the export business is established with your three distributors, they will need you as the main connection. Establish yourself as the main connection to both your suppliers and your distributors.

Example Two
Strategy Twenty-Four in action (against you)

You are in the business of aged care and you export your latest technology to China. You perceive your company has positioned itself on the leading edge in the aged care sector, helping the elderly live independently in a retirement village as opposed to an aged care home with assisted living. Your company makes devices that monitor three critical vital life signs. These are blood pressure, sugar levels, and any abnormal heart rhythms. These devices are very small and easy to use. You have been exporting to a large retirement village company just outside Shanghai for almost five years, and they seem to be loyal to you. Your product is of a very high standard and you have also spent a lot of effort developing solid *guanxi*. The retirement village that you export your product to also acts as a distributor to sell these devices to other retirement villages across China. This has been a good situation, as you only have to deal with one company and they have strong connections in this sector. As this is a niche market, you conclude that it would be difficult for someone who is not Chinese to locate other distributors, so this situation suits you well. You have been making two trips per year to China to visit your client. You are aware that your product is slightly more expensive than your competitors. However, you know that your product is of high quality and your client has never questioned the price. During these visits you meet with the senior management and marketing team and explain to them how the devices work. You thought this was important because you wanted them to have a deeper understanding of the product. So you share not just what the device does, but also the technical aspects of how it works.

In the fifth year of business there is a large retirement village exhibition in your home city. Your client in China is interested in attending this exhibition and you feel this is an excellent opportunity to show them your offices and your city, and escort them to the exhibition. You have been to China many times and they have been excellent hosts, so you would like to return the hospitality. Three people from the company visit your offices and laboratory, and they are very impressed. They spend a whole day visiting your premises. You then take them sightseeing for two days, and after that they visit the exhibition for two days. These people speak very good English, which makes it easy for you to introduce them to people at the exhibition.

After your client returns to China you realise that their next order is a significant lower quantity. When you attend a local retirement village networking function, one of your competitors tells you that they have just been given a large order from a company in China, and after asking a few questions you realise they are dealing with your client. This is a big surprise because you thought you had a solid client and that they would be loyal to you. The client applied Strategy Twenty-Four by '*borrowing your resources*,' which were your connections and your technical knowledge. They were able to approach your competitors with knowledge of the technology and therefore ask the right questions. These competitors were also selling the same technology at a cheaper price than you. After one month your client contacts you and '*they are using the resources to turn on you when you lent them these resources in the first place*.' These resources are your connections in your home country, where you introduced them to people at the exhibitions, and also the technology you taught them about which explained how your devices work. When they contact you they request to buy your devices at a cheaper price. Strategy Twenty-Four has been successfully applied and you are now in a position where you will need to reduce your prices otherwise you will lose all business from this company. Also, all of your other exports in China go through this business, as you only have this one distributor, and so you need to keep them onside.

Example Two
Guarding yourself against Strategy Twenty-Four

In this situation, to guard against Strategy Twenty-Four being successfully applied against you, it would have been wise to keep a better awareness of market prices. A complacent attitude about your clients remaining loyal to you when cheaper products become available can be very risky when dealing with China. With some good market research the product may have been able to be modified with less expensive components, and therefore sold at a cheaper price to remain competitive.

There was no need to give the team in China so much information, as this gave them enough knowledge to go somewhere else and ask the right technical questions, which in this case was your competitive edge. They could have been given much less information. Working out how much to tell people when you deal with China is important. There is a line. Take care not to go over that line. More observations of how your guests behaved at the exhibition would have provided an idea of what was happening. Debriefing with them after the exhibition about what they liked and if there was anything you needed to modify about your product would also have been useful. It is a good idea not to assume that they are attending the exhibition just to see you. It is likely they will have another purpose to their visit. Loyalty is important. Even so, when it comes to price they will search out other options. Visiting the exhibition was a perfect opportunity for your distributor to do this. By not thinking through all the layers and putting guards in place, this aged care device business was vulnerable to the application of Strategy Twenty-Four.

Key Points when Strategy Twenty-Four is used against you

- Do your research to understand why your Chinese clients are forming alliances with you or other contacts.
- Be careful how much technical product information you share with your distributors.
- When combining the resources of other companies to export a product to China, always be the main contact and keep the control.

EXAMPLE THREE
Enacting Strategy Twenty-Four

You own and design a product that is a unique and complex piece of machinery for irrigation pumping. This machinery is used specifically in dry areas and desert regions. You import the components to construct this piece of machinery. Before beginning the import process you spent a year making sure that the three factories you selected all understood the drawings to the standard you required. You cleverly chose three factories to work with because this reduced the likelihood that your product could be copied. Each factory produces a different component that is sent back to your own country, where you assemble the final product. This means your intellectual property is as safe as you can make it. Three years have gone by and this arrangement has worked very well. The product is of a high standard and you have good strong *guanxi* with all of the factories. Two of the factories you deal with manufacture all the constituents of your components, whereas the other factory buys the constituent elements from another source to assemble the component they export to you.

To apply Strategy Twenty-Four you request that this factory takes you to where the constituent parts are being made so you can learn about all the different stages of your product's manufacturing processes. By doing this you are applying Strategy Twenty-Four. In the application of Strategy Twenty-Four you '*borrow the resources of the factory you are dealing with*', by finding out about the constituent elements that they are buying from elsewhere. The resources you borrow are the introductions to the factory that manufactures the constituent parts, and with the application of Strategy Twenty-Four it becomes obvious that you can go directly to the manufacturers and get these constituent parts for a cheaper price. You do not want to completely sever ties with the original factory that you have been dealing with, as they have always produced a high-quality product and delivered on time. Instead, you split the order for this component between the original factory and the factory that makes the constituent elements. By doing this you get half of your product order for a lower price and still retain a relationship with the original factory.

Negotiating in a Western Environment

Example Four
Enacting Strategy Twenty-Four

Imagine that you have been working in graphic design for some time and you have worked your way up to a management level. You are now ready to take your career further, but think it is unlikely a promotion will become available at your current company in the near future. You decide that you would like to become a freelance designer and go into business for yourself. You are sure that you have the technical skills and expertise to do well on your own. However, you are unsure how to go about setting up a new business. You implement Strategy Twenty-Four to '*borrow the resources of an ally*' by taking a job with a small graphic design business where you will have a lot of contact with the business owner and be able to observe what it takes to run your own business. You work in that job to develop the knowledge and skills you need, so that you are able to put them to work when you set up you own business.

Key Points when using Strategy Twenty-Four

- When importing products from China, to reduce the risk of your intellectual property being copied, spread the importing of the components across more than one supplier.
- Understand where your product is made, because your supplier may be buying your product from an outsourced supplier. Research whether you can go straight to the source, in order to lower your costs.
- Identify what skills you need for your future career development and then find an ally from whom you can learn these skills.

Your Next Steps

Having just finished reading *Bewilder the Dragon*, here are some suggestions for your next steps:

- Now I can plan my approach when I am negotiating in any situation.
- The 36 Strategies will help me when communicating with Chinese people.
- I will share this knowledge with my colleagues.
- I want to read *The Dao of Negotiation* series. I'll find them at **www.leoniemckeon.com**
- I will contact Leonie to:
  - Help me think completely differently about my business development challenges.
  - Deliver a presentation for my next conference or other event.
  - Deliver 36 Strategies workshops to my team.
- Because **Pronounce Mandarin - The Easy Way** is perfect for beginners, I will learn how to correctly pronounce Chinese names and some useful Mandarin Chinese words and phrases via **www.pronouncemandarin.com**

Go to **www.leoniemckeon.com** for more information about the 36 Strategies. Leonie has several informative videos and blogs to help you further your understanding of how to negotiate in any business environment.

WHAT PEOPLE SAY ABOUT WORKING
WITH LEONIE MCKEON

BEC HARDY WINES

"I can't tell you how much you have given our family, and me personally, through your insights about the 36 Chinese Strategies. Understanding how the 36 Chinese Strategies are applied in Chinese business culture was the lightbulb moment which has led to such revenue growth, opportunities and personal growth. This has been one of the great, exciting professional and personal journeys and achievements of my life. Thanks again."

Richard Dolan, Joint Managing Director

HATCH, Western Australia

"Anyone who has the pleasure of having dealings with China and the Chinese will find Leonie's 36 Chinese Strategies workshops invaluable. The workshops were eye-opening and had the right amount of humour and personal stories to more than keep our attention."

Denis Pesci, PDG Hub Director, Western Australia

Fletcher Building

"From a personal perspective, Leonie was instrumental to our Chinese cultural program developed for the Super Retail Group. The target audience for the workshop was our Management and Leaders from Logistics, Marketing and Category. In organising the program for the team, I found Leonie incredibly resourceful, totally understood the brief and built value-add to the program. Often you don't know what you don't know so great to have a Subject Matter Expert to guide and shape a very successful program."

Shirley Brown, Capability Development Manager – Australian Distribution

Australian American Fulbright Commission

"The Art of Negotiation – 36 Strategies derived from 'The Art of War' workshop delivered by Leonie at the Australian Institute of Company Directors (AICD) challenged conventional thinking."

Peter de Cure, Chairman, Australian American Fulbright Commission

Kmart

"The training that Leonie provided to our team was excellent. The program was practical, delivered with context, and opened the team members' minds to learning more about how to do better business in China. I have no doubt that what we have learned will be applied and will provide great outcomes for our business. Leonie has also provided a great personal development opportunity for members of our team."

Matthew Webber, International Supply Chain Manager

The Dao of Negotiation
The Path between Eastern Strategies and Western Minds

		Strategy Number
Book One – *Tame the Tiger*	Advantageous Strategies	1, 2, 3, 4, 5, 6
Book Two – *Deceive the Dragon*	Opportunistic Strategies	7, 8, 9, 10, 11, 12,
Book Three – *Lure the Tiger*	Strategies for Attack	13, 14, 15, 16, 17, 18
Book Four – *Bewilder the Dragon*	Confusion Strategies	19, 20, 21, 22, 23, 24
Book Five – *Endure the Tiger*	Strategies for Gaining Ground	25, 26, 27, 28, 29, 30
Book Six – *Flee the Dragon*	Strategies for Desperate Situations	31, 32, 33, 34, 35, 36

The Dao of Negotiation:
The Path between Eastern Strategies and Western Minds

by Leonie McKeon

More Control, More Success, More Wins!

Based on *The Art of War*, *The Dao of Negotiation* series unmask the 36 Strategies used in Chinese culture and business.

This incredible series of 6 books provide invaluable tips for any business person looking to improve their overall negotiation skills, as well as become better at negotiating with Chinese People.

Discover how you can use this ancient wisdom for more business success.

www.leoniemckeon.com